Christmas Album

Photo Album Instructions

There are 24 picture frame pages in this album. You may slide your photographs in through the top of the page and center it into the picture frame. Turn the page and slide your next photograph in the same manner. Your photographs will be back to back inside the picture frame. These picture frames are designed for 4" x 6" photographs ("Supersize" snapshots).

Designed by Roni Akmon

We would like to thank the following for their permission
to reproduce certain illustrations in this book:
Fine Art Photographs, Bridgeman Art Library, and Picturepoint Library.
The Gingerbread Mansion is by Heather Nixon.
Picture Frame Illustrations by Sue Rother.

Efforts have been made to find the copyright holders of material used in this publication. We apologize for any omissions or errors and will be pleased to include the appropriate acknowledgments in future editions.

ISBN 0-926684-05-1

Published by Blushing Rose Publishing
P.O. Box 2238
San Anselmo, CA 94979
Distributed by Eclectic Press Inc.

Printed and bound in Singapore

Christmas Album

a family keepsake & photo album
of Christmas. A six year journal.

For: _____

With Love From: _____

Date: _____

Designed by Roni Akmon
Written by Nancy Cogan

Blushing Rose Publishing
San Anselmo, California

A Visit from St. Nicholas

Twas the night before Christmas, when all through the house—Not a creature was stirring, not even a mouse; The stockings were hung by the chimney with care, In hopes that St. Nicholas soon would be there; The children were nestled all snug in their beds, While visions of sugar-plums danced in their heads; And mamma in her kerchief, and I in my cap, Had just settled our brains for a long winter's nap—When out on the lawn there arose such a clatter, I sprang from my bed to see what was the matter. Away to the window I flew like a flash, Tore open the shutters, and threw up the sash. The moon, on the breast of the new-fallen snow, Gave the luster of midday to objects below; When, what to my wondering eyes should appear, But a miniature sleigh and eight tiny reindeer, With a little old driver, so lively and quick, I knew in a moment it must be St. Nick. More rapid than eagles his coursers they came, And he whistled, and shouted, and called them by name: "Now, Dasher! now, Dancer! now, Prancer and Vixen! On, Comet! on, Cupid! on, Donner and Blitzen! "To the top of the porch! to the top of the wall! Now dash away! dash away! dash away all!" As dry leaves that before the wild hurricane fly, When they meet with an obstacle, mount to the sky; So up to the house-top the coursers they flew—With the sleigh full of toys, and St. Nicholas too. And then, in a twinkling, I heard on the roof—The prancing and pawing of each little hoof—As I drew in my head, and was turning around, Down the chimney St. Nicholas came with a bound. He was dressed all in fur, from his head to his foot, And his clothers were all tarnished with ashes and soot; A bundle of toys he had flung on his back, and he looked like a peddlar just opening his pack. His eyes—how they twinkled; his dimples, how merry! His cheeks were like roses, his nose like a cherry! His droll little mouth was drawn up like bow, And the beard of his chin was as white as the snow; The stump of a pipe he held tight in his teeth, And the smoke it encircled his head like a wreath; He had a broad face and a little round belly—That shook, when he laughed, like a bowl full of jelly. He was chubby and plump, a right jolly old elf, And I laughed when I saw him, in spite of myself; A wink of his eye and a twist of his head—Soon gave me to know I had nothing to dread; He spoke not a word, but went straight to his work, And filled all the stockings; then turned with a jerk, And laying his finger aside of his nose, And giving a nod, up the chimney he rose; He sprang to his sleigh, to his team give a whistle, And away they all few like the down of a thistle. But I heard him exclaim, ere he drove out of sight, "Happy Christmas to all, and to all a good night!"

CLEMENT CLARK MOORE—1823

Christmas Year of _____

Christmas Gatherings

Holiday Visits & Visitors—Family and Friends

Holiday Parties and Events

Christmas Menus

Christmas comes but once a year, and when it comes it brings good cheer.

Christmas Eve Menu _____

_____

_____

_____

Christmas Day Menu _____

_____

_____

_____

Christmas Dinner _____

_____

_____

_____

Christmas Card List

We seem too busy every day to say the things we want to say;
Our deepest thoughts we seem to hide until we reach the Christmas tide.
'Tis then we send to friends again,
In happy words the old refrain—'Very Merry Christmas'

—Verse from a Victorian Christmas Card

Christmas Cards

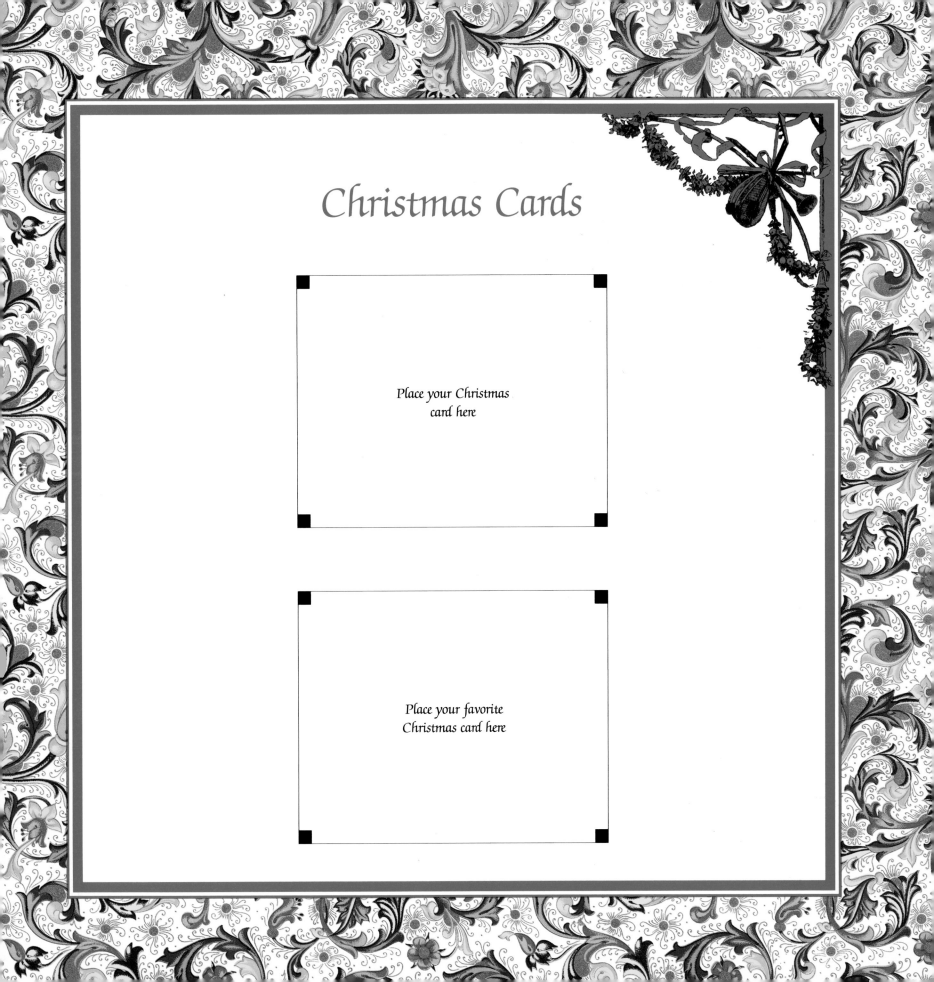

Place your Christmas
card here

Place your favorite
Christmas card here

Photographs

Photographs

Welcome Christmas

With Holly and Ivy so green and so gay,
We deck up our houses as fresh as the day;
With bay and rosemary and laurel complete;
and everyone now is a King in conceit.

—Anonymous, 17th Century

Special Christmas Presents _____

_____

_____

_____

_____

Christmas Tree & Decorations _____

_____

_____

_____

Special Moments We Will Remember _____

_____

_____

_____

New Years Celebrations

When as you sing of Christmas cheer, And welcome in the bright new year, And feast and laugh and dance and play, And open gifts on Christmas Day, Pause as you hear the angels' words, And don't neglect the little birds.

—Anonymous, 1909

New Years Parties _____

_____

_____

_____

New Years Resolutions _____

_____

_____

_____

WISHING YOU A HAPPY NEW YEAR

The Christmas Tree

The Christmas tree was an old German custom. The tradition was originally brought to England by King George I. The tree was placed in the middle of a table and decorated brilliantly with lighted candles, sweets, fruits and bright trinkets.

In 1941 Prince Albert put up a large Christmas tree at Windsor Castle, as he remembered the pleasure of this custom from his childhood in Germany. The large decorated Christmas tree soon became very fashionable in Victorian England.

In America, the Christmas tree had already become popular due to the German immigrants that settled here.

Today, we continue the tradition with trees alight in the windows along the street, with their shining color and their sweet smell, a symbol of our Christmas celebration.

Christmas Year of _____

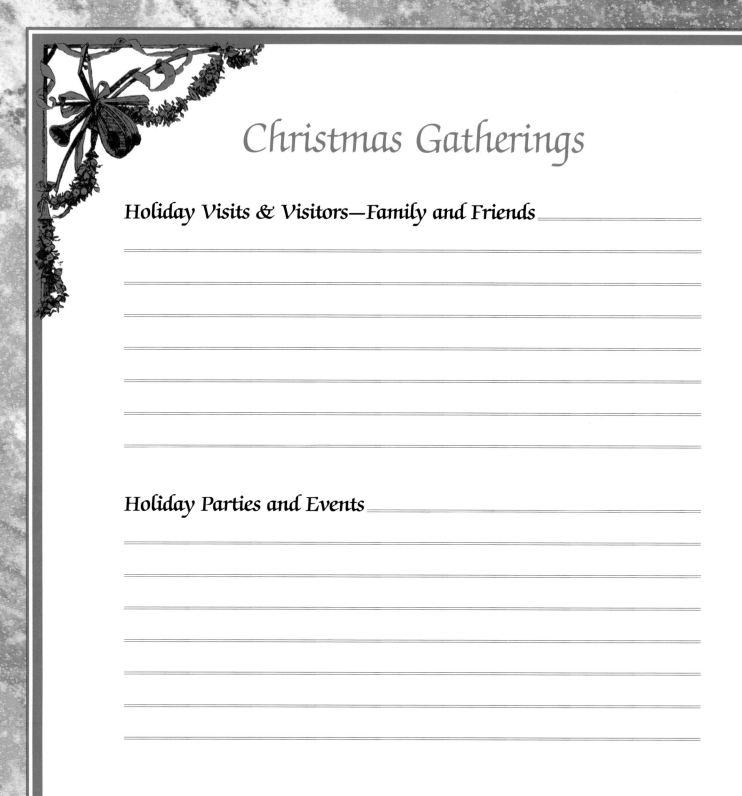

Christmas Gatherings

Holiday Visits & Visitors—Family and Friends _____

_____

_____

_____

_____

_____

_____

Holiday Parties and Events _____

_____

_____

_____

_____

_____

_____

Christmas Menus

 ow thrice welcome, Christmas, which brings us good cheer; Minced pies and plum porridge, good ale and strong beer; With pig, goose and capon, the best that may be, So well doth the weather and our stomachs agree.

—Poor Richards Almanac, 1695

Christmas Eve Menu

_____

_____

_____

_____

Christmas Day Menu

_____

_____

_____

_____

Christmas Dinner

_____

_____

_____

_____

I have been looking on, this evening, at a merry company of children assembled round that pretty German toy, a Christmas tree. The tree was planted in the middle of a great round table, and towered high above their heads. It was brilliantly lighted by a multitude of little tapers; and everywhere sparkled and glittered with bright objects. There were rosy-cheeked dolls, hiding behind the green leaves; and there were real watches (with movable hands, at least, and an endless capacity of being wound up) dangling from innumerable twigs; there were French-polished tables, chairs, bedsteads, wardrobes, eight day clocks, and various other articles of domestic furniture (wonderfully made, in tin, at Wolverhampton), perched among the boughs, as if in preparation for some fairy housekeeping; there were jolly broadfaced men, more agreeable in appearance than many real men—and no wonder, for their heads took off, and showed them to be full of sugar-plums; there were fiddles and drums . . . there were trinkets for the elder girls, far brighter than any grown-up gold and jewels; there were baskets and pincushions in all devices . . . imitation apples, pears and walnuts, crammed with surprises; in short, as a pretty child, before me, delightedly whispered to another pretty child, "There was everything, and more."

—Christmas Stories, Charles Dickens

Christmas Cards

Place your Christmas
card here

Place your favorite
Christmas card here

Photographs

The Fir Tree

The Fir Tree was put into a great tub filled with sand . . . The servants, and the young ladies also decked it out. On one branch they hung little nets, cut out of colored paper; every net was filled with sweetmeats; golden apples and walnuts hung down as if they grew there, and more than a hundred little candles, red, white and blue, were fastened to the different boughs. Dolls that looked exactly like real people—the Tree had never seen such before—swung among the foliage, and high on the summit of the Tree was fixed a tinsel star. It was splendid, particularly splendid. 'This evening,' said all, 'this evening it will shine.'

—Hans Christian Andersen

Special Christmas Presents

_____

_____

_____

_____

Christmas Tree & Decorations

_____

_____

_____

_____

Special Moments We Will Remember

_____

_____

_____

_____

New Years Celebrations

Ring out the old, ring in the new,
Ring, happy bells, across the snow;
The year is going, let him go;
Ring out the false, ring in the true.

Ring out the grief that saps the mind,
For those that here we see no more;
Ring out the feud of rich and poor,
Ring in redress to all mankind.

Ring out old shapes of foul disease;
Ring out the narrowing lust of gold;
Ring out the thousand wars of old,
Ring in the thousand years of peace.

—Alfred Lord Tennyson–1851

New Years Parties

_____

_____

_____

_____

New Years Resolutions

_____

_____

_____

_____

The Gathering of Mistletoe, Holly and the Ivy

 vergreens have always played an important part in our celebrations throughout history. To the early Romans evergreens meant good luck. During the winter they decorated their homes with sprigs of holly and ivy.

Pine branches were used for their sweet smell, holly for its medicinal properties, and ivy was a sign of good cheer.

Mistletoe was linked with old Druid sacrificial rites. They would gather it from the woods with much ceremony and their followers would adorn themselves with sprigs of the mistletoe. After the ceremonial rites, those in attendance, would take home sprigs of mistletoe to decorate their dwellings as an emblem of good fortune. The old superstition of kissing under the mistletoe was derived from this belief.

Christmas Year of _____

Christmas Gatherings

Holiday Visits & Visitors—Family and Friends _____

_____

_____

_____

_____

_____

_____

_____

Holiday Parties and Events _____

_____

_____

_____

_____

_____

_____

Christmas Menus

A Victorian Feast

eaped up on the floor, to form a kind of throne, were turkeys, geese, game, poultry, brawn, great joints of meat, suckling pigs, long wreaths of sausage, mince-pies, plum-puddings, barrels of oysters, red-hot chestnuts, cherry-cheeked apples, juicy oranges, luscious pears, immense twelfth cakes, and seething bowls of punch, that made the chamber dim with their delicious steam.

—A Christmas Carol, Charles Dickens (1843)

Christmas Eve Menu

Christmas Day Menu

Christmas Dinner

I don't know what day of the month it is," said Scrooge. "I don't know how long I have been among the Spirits. I don't know anything. I'm quite a baby. Never mind; I don't care. I'd rather be a baby. Hallo! Whoop! Hallo here!"

He was checked in his transports by the churches ringing out the lustiest peals he had ever heard. Clash, clash, hammer; ding, dong, bell. Bell, dong, ding; hammer, clang, clash! Oh, glorious, glorious!

Running to the window, he opened it, and put his head out. No fog, no mist; clear, bright, jovial, stirring, cold; cold piping for the blood to dance to; golden sunlight; Heavenly sky; sweet fresh air; merry bells. Oh, glorious, glorious!

"What's today?" cried Scrooge, calling downward to a boy in Sunday clothes, who perhaps had loitered in to look about him.

"Eh?" returned the boy, with all his might of wonder.

"What's today, my fine fellow?" said Scrooge.

"Today!" replied the boy. "Why, CHRISTMAS DAY."

A Christmas Carol—Charles Dickens

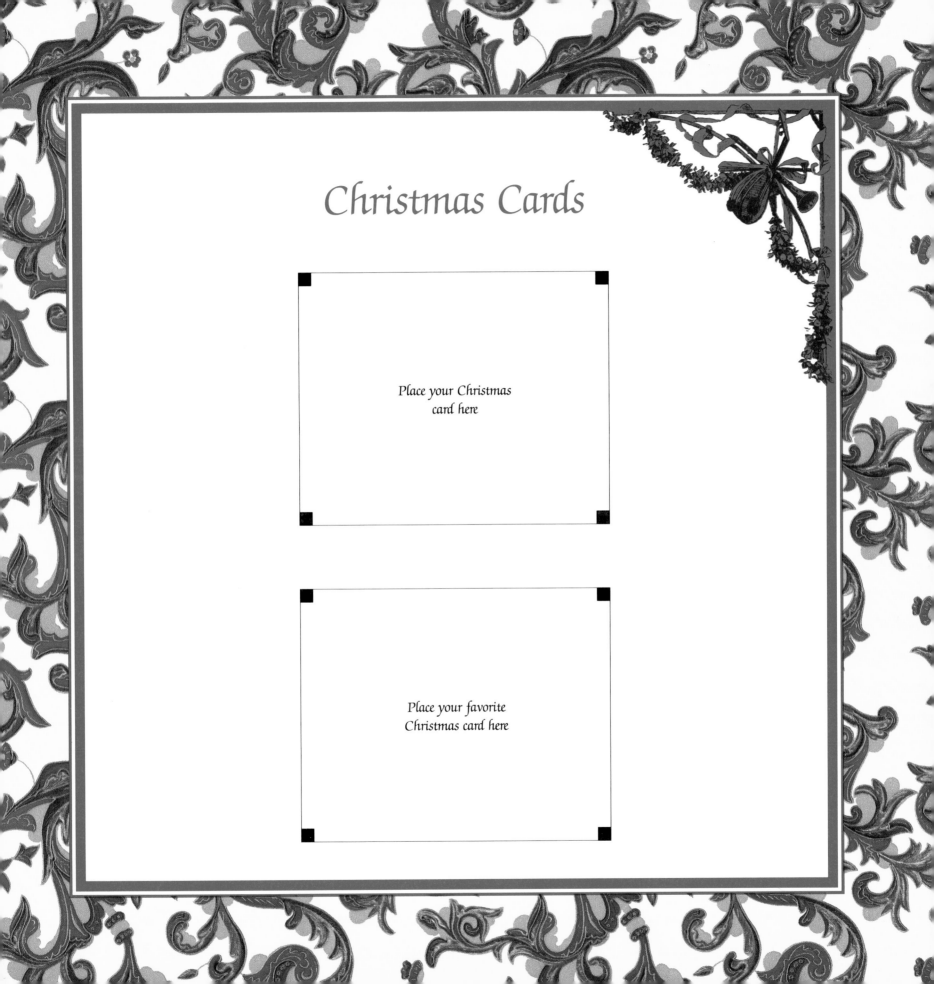

Christmas Cards

Place your Christmas
card here

Place your favorite
Christmas card here

Photographs

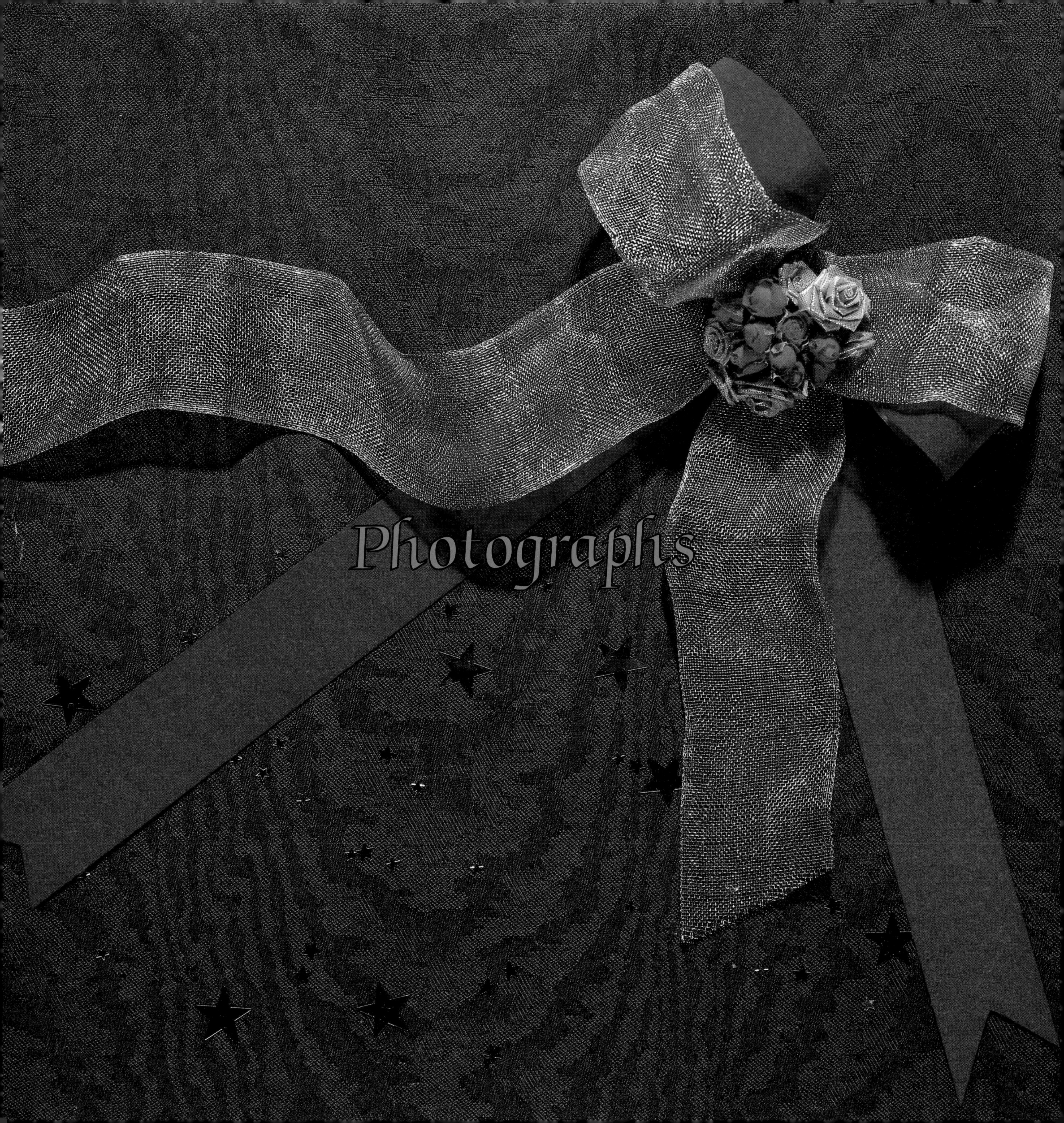
Photographs

Our Christmas At Home

But give me holly, Bold and jolly,
Honest, prickly, Shining holly.
Pluck me holly, Leaf and berry
For the day when I make merry.
—Christina Rossetti

Special Christmas Presents _____

_____

_____

_____

_____

Christmas Tree & Decorations _____

_____

_____

_____

Special Moments We Will Remember _____

_____

_____

_____

New Years Celebrations

Deck the hall with boughs of holly, 'Tis the season to be jolly,
Don we now our gay apparel, Troll the ancient yule-tide carol.
Fast away the old year passes, Hail the new, ye lads and lasses,
Sing we joyous all together, Heedless of the wind and weather.

—A traditional Welsh Carol

New Years Parties _____

_____

_____

_____

New Years Resolutions _____

_____

_____

_____

WISHING YOU A   HAPPY NEW YEAR

Christmas Cards

We owe to Victorian England another beloved tradition—that of sending Christmas cards. In 1846 Sir Henry Cole, the first director of the Victoria and Albert Museum, designed and printed the first Christmas Card. In the 1860's, new developments in printing which lowered costs and the introduction of printed matter going as first class mail made the sending of Christmas cards extremely popular.

Victorian Christmas cards were ornate with lace, flowers, and satin and often were 3-dimensional. The typical scenes, as we know today of Santa Claus, Christmas trees, Nativity, Angels, etc. were orignated in the Victorian era.

Christmas Year of _____

Christmas Gatherings

Holiday Visits & Visitors—Family and Friends

_____

_____

_____

_____

_____

_____

Holiday Parties and Events

_____

_____

_____

_____

_____

_____

Christmas Menus

Brawn, pudding and souse, and good mustard withal, Beef, mutton, and pork shred pies of the best, Pig, veal, goose, and capon, and turkey well dressed, Cheese, apples and nuts, jolly carols to hear, As them in the country is counted as good cheer

—Thomas Tusser, 1524-1580

Christmas Eve Menu

Christmas Day Menu

Christmas Dinner

Gingerbread Victorian Mansion

Gingerbread

2 lbs. 10 oz. flour
3 Tsp. baking soda
2 Tbl. cloves & ginger
4 Tbl. cinnamon
15 oz. butter or margarine
15 oz. sugar
1 lb. 2 oz. corn syrup
3/4 cup milk

Preheat the oven to 400°. In a large bowl, blend together flour, baking soda, & spices. In a saucepan melt the butter, sugar & corn syrup over a low heat (not over 110°). Add the milk & stir, then pour into dry ingredients. Blend until well mixed. Put mixture into refrigerator overnight. Knead dough & roll out 1/8" thick on a floured board. Put on pattern piece and using a pizza cutter, cut into shape and bake on a greased cookie sheet for 10-15 minutes. Bake until the gingerbread is a rich brown and is well cooked.

Other Materials Needed

24 x 18 in. board, covered in green foil
4 candy canes
12 oz. chocolate-covered raisins for the chimney
1 lb. red and green small gumdrops.
48 lace decorations (piped royal icing onto wax paper with nozzle tip)
6 oz. chocolate non-pareils.
1/2 cup confectioners sugar
Edible gold leaf (optional)
Transparent cellophane for windows

Royal Icing

2 lbs. confectioners sugar, sifted
6 Tbls. meringue powder
2/3 cups warm water

Use a clean, grease-free mixing bowl. Combine sugar and the meringue powder. Add the water and beat until the icing forms a peak. 9-11 minutes approx. with a mixer. Cover the icing with a damp cloth while you are making gingerbread house. Color 4 cups of the icing in white, 1-1/2 cups of it in green, 1/2 cup of it in brown, and 1/2 cup of it in red.

Gingerbread Shapes Needed for Mansion

Gingerbread Instructions

Enlarge the shapes on the opposite page and cut out card templates. Roll and cut the gingerbread pieces and bake them. (You will need 2 of the long rectangle shapes shown, with the door and window cut-outs.)

Pipe Royal Icing dots around windows on inside and stick pieces of transparent paper in place. Turn over and decorate edges of windows.

Cover a 24" x 18" board with green foil paper.

Starting with the plain back wall, pipe a line of icing on bottom and sides and stick to board. Add the two pointed sides and hold in place to stick. Add front section of wall "glueing" bottom and sides in place. Reinforce inner joints with more "glue." Pipe a line of icing along top edges, then attach back roof piece, making sure that the smaller cut-out section is on the far back corner of the house. Attach the front roof piece and position so that the large cut-out piece is in the front.

Find pieces for side porch. "Glue" the sides and front onto the side of the house and position it off center. Pipe top edges with icing and "glue" on roof pieces. Pipe a line down center of roof.

"Glue" on front doors and side porch door leaving slightly ajar. Pipe all around edges and add door handle dots.

Now construct the front extension: "glue" sides onto house and board fitting it into the cut-out piece of roof, then position front and "glue." Run a line of icing along top edges and secure roof pieces, then run a line of icing along the top seam.

Sandwich the two chimney pieces together with icing, then attach to side of house with icing, fitting it into cut-out section.

Decorate tops of doors with candy and trails of green holly and red berry dots of icing.

Place base of verandah in front of house; fit snugly. It may be necessary to trim gingerbread to fit. "Glue" in place.

Cut candy canes to desired length. "Glue" into place; decorate with trails of holly. Pipe dots on top of candy canes and attach top of verandah on candy canes and "glue" to house.

Stick shutters onto outside of windows and decorate.

Spread chimney with brown icing and stick chocolate covered raisins or similar candy to represent stones.

Cover roof and top of verandah with layer of white icing and decorate with rows of red and green candies or gingerbread hearts or as desired. Decorate trim of house with zig-zags made with star tube.

Using stiff Royal Icing, pipe icicles dropping from roof line. Spread icing around house for landscaping. Add a gingerbread or chocolate disc pathway to front and side of house.

Decorate yard with trees, bushes and snowman. Spread a layer of white icing on the board for the yard. Place chocolate non-pareils for the path. Make the tree by piping green icing onto the ice cream cone. Use green icing with a med. star tip. Start at the bottom and work up. Pipe out a snowman with a round tip and place it on the board near the pathway.

To finish, sift a dusting of powdered sugar over house and garden to give the impression of freshly fallen snow.

Photographs

Photographs

Gift Giving

"Christmas won't be Christmas without any presents . . . "
—Louisa May Alcott, Little Women

Special Christmas Presents

_____

_____

_____

_____

_____

Christmas Tree & Decorations

_____

_____

_____

_____

Special Moments We Will Remember

_____

_____

_____

_____

New Years Celebrations

We wish you a Merry Christmas
We wish you a Merry Christmas
We wish you a Merry Christmas
And a Happy New Year!

—An English Carol

New Years Parties

New Years Resolutions

Christmas Carols

In the Nineteenth Century carol-singing gained new popularity in England and America. Some of our most popular Christmas Carols: "We the Three Kings" and "Away in a Manger" were composed at that time in America.

The early carol singers were known as 'Wassailers'. They went from house to house singing carols during the Christmas season. They gave each householder sprigs of mistletoe and holly and carried a Wassail-bowl filled with hot spiced ale flavored with sugar and apples. The Waissailers would be invited in to drink to their hosts health from the Wassail-bowl. The hosts would then fill the bowl up again and sometimes would give them gifts of money or food.

The word 'Wassail' is from an Anglo-Saxon toast, 'Drink-Hail', meaning 'Good Health'!

Christmas Year of _____

Christmas Gatherings

Holiday Visits & Visitors—Family and Friends _____

_____

_____

_____

_____

_____

Holiday Parties and Events _____

_____

_____

_____

_____

_____

Christmas Menus

Christmas is coming, the Goose is getting Fat,
Please put a penny in the old man's hat.
If you haven't a penny, a ha' penny will do,
If you haven't a penny—God bless you!

—a traditional Children's Rhyme

Christmas Eve Menu

Christmas Day Menu

Christmas Dinner

Joy To The World

2. Joy to the World! the Saviour reigns,
   Let men their songs employ,
   While field and floods, rocks, hills and plains,
   Repeat the sounding joy.

3. He rules the world with truth and grace,
   And makes the nations prove
   The glories of His righteousness,
   And wonders of His love.

Christmas Cards

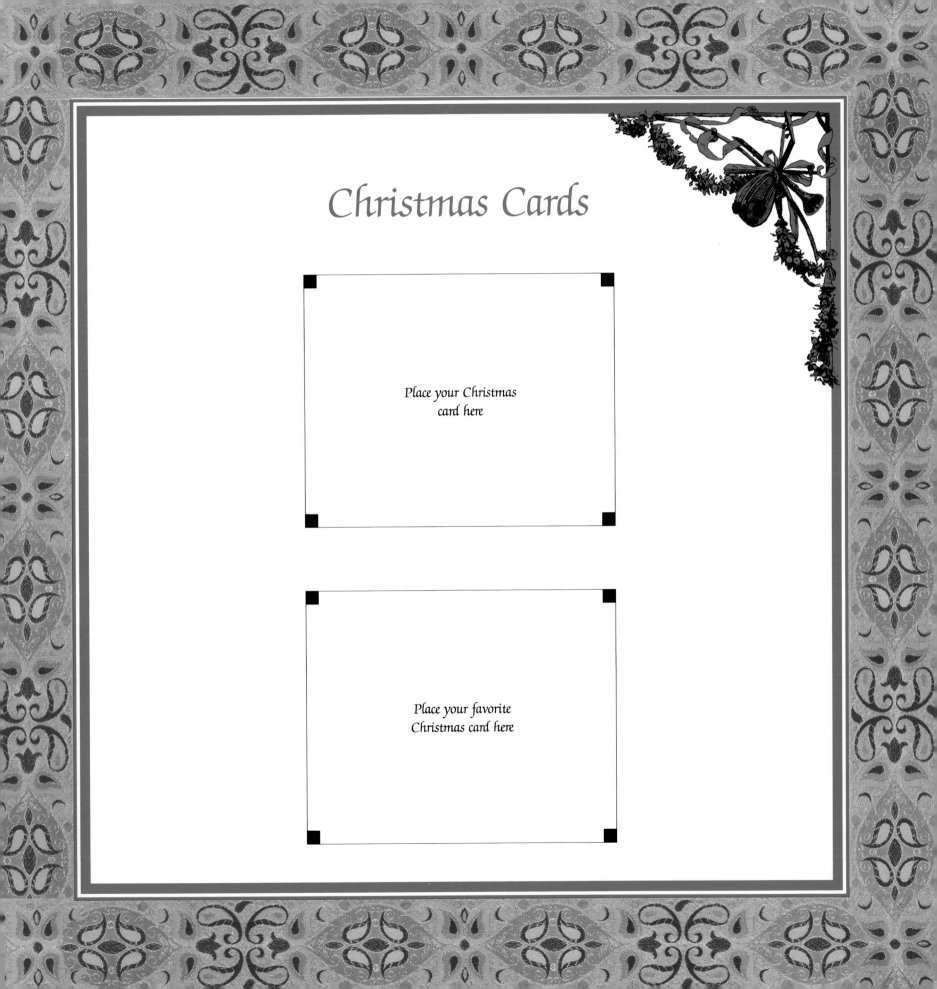

Place your Christmas
card here

Place your favorite
Christmas card here

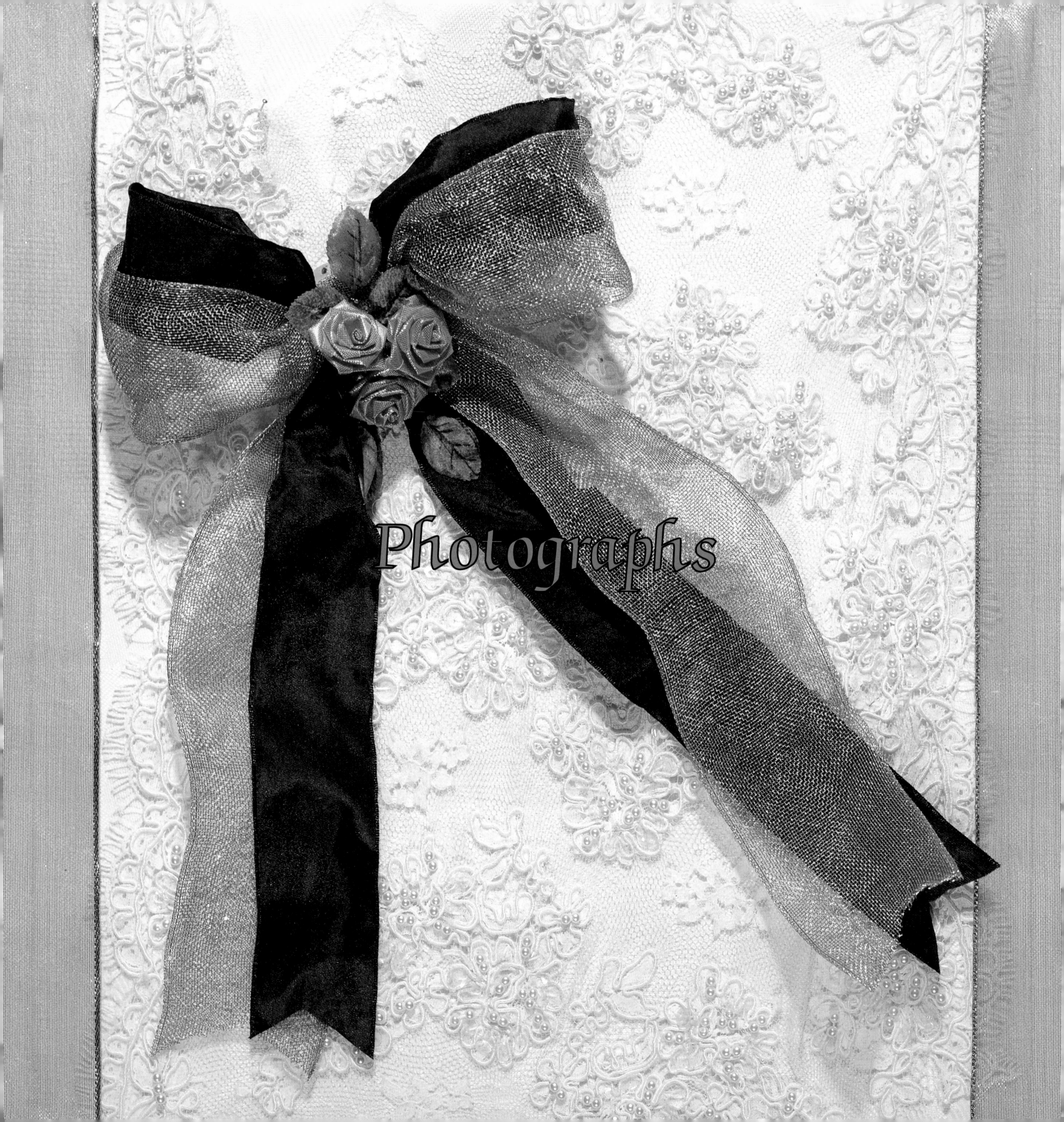
Photographs

Photographs

My Gift

Special Christmas Presents _____

_____

_____

_____

Christmas Tree & Decorations _____

_____

_____

_____

Special Moments We Will Remember _____

_____

_____

_____

New Years Celebrations

H ere we come a-wassailing, Among the leaves so green,
Here we come a wandering; So fair to be seen;
Love and joy come to you, And to your wassail too,
And God bless you, and send you
A happy New Year, And God send you, A happy New Year.

—Wassail Song, Anonymous

New Years Parties

_____

_____

_____

New Years Resolutions

_____

_____

_____

_____

WISHING YOU A   HAPPY NEW YEAR

The Christmas Stocking

All children delight in receiving small gifts in their Christmas stocking. The legend goes—On Christmas Eve, St. Nicholas threw gold coins down the chimney into stockings that were hanging by the fire to dry.

Christmas Year of _____

Christmas Gatherings

Holiday Visits & Visitors—Family and Friends _____

_____

_____

_____

_____

_____

Holiday Parties and Events _____

_____

_____

_____

_____

_____

_____

Twelve Days of Christmas

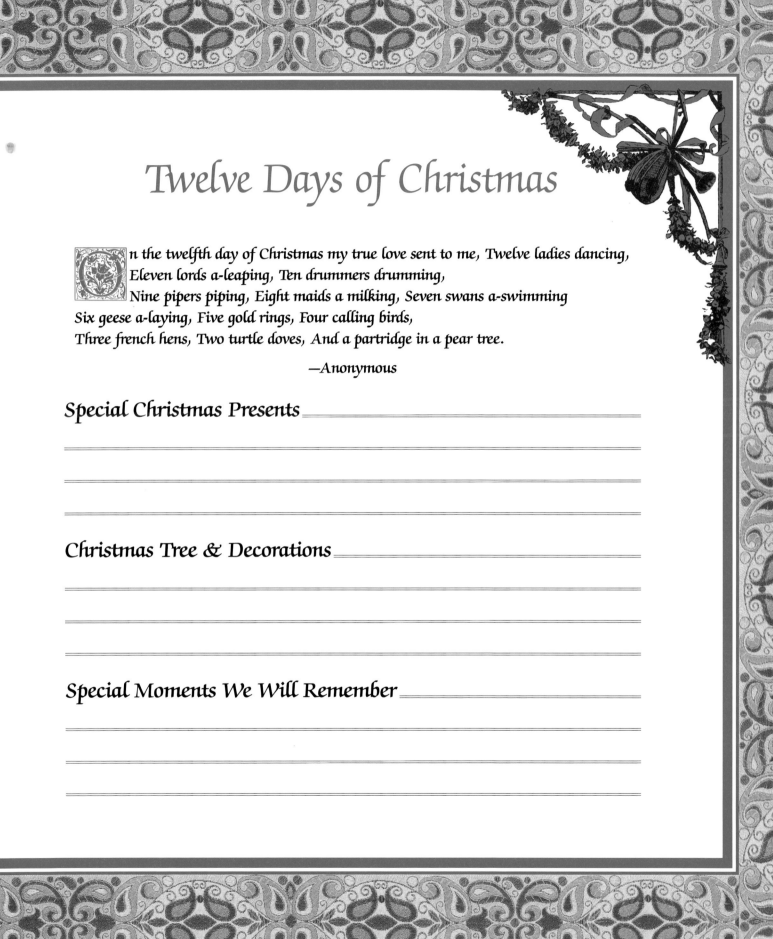

On the twelfth day of Christmas my true love sent to me, Twelve ladies dancing,
Eleven lords a-leaping, Ten drummers drumming,
Nine pipers piping, Eight maids a milking, Seven swans a-swimming
Six geese a-laying, Five gold rings, Four calling birds,
Three french hens, Two turtle doves, And a partridge in a pear tree.

—Anonymous

Special Christmas Presents _____

_____

_____

_____

Christmas Tree & Decorations _____

_____

_____

_____

Special Moments We Will Remember _____

_____

_____

_____

New Years Celebrations

Should auld acquaintance be forgot, And never brought to mind,
Should auld acquaintance be forgot, And days of Auld Lang Syne?
Chorus: For Auld Lang Syne, my dear, For Auld Lang Syne,
We'll take a cup o'kindness yet, For Auld Lang Syne

—Robert Burns

New Years Parties _____

_____

_____

New Years Resolutions _____

_____

_____

_____

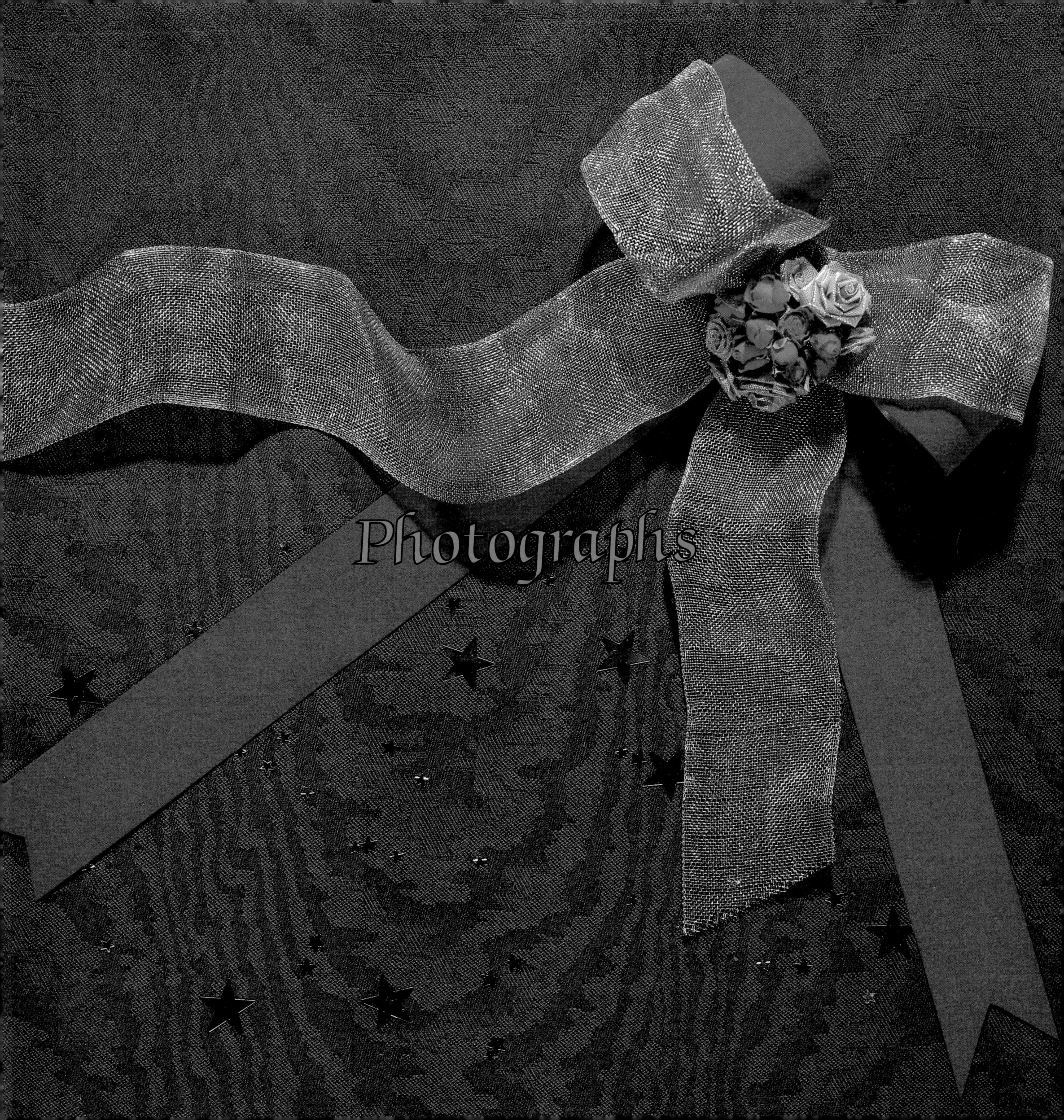
Photographs

A Blessing

od bless the master of this house,
The mistress also,
And all the little children
That round the table go:

And all your kin and kinsfolk,
That dwell both far and near;
I wish you a merry Christmas
and a happy New Year.

—Anonymous, 17th Century